HOW TO MAKE LIP BALM

A Beginners step by step Guide to making highly natural lip balm in 20 days.

Simple whiz

COPYRIGHT/DISCLAIMER

Disclaimer / Copyright © 2024 by Simple Whiz . All rights reserved.

No part of this book may be copied, distributed, or transmitted in any way without the author's prior written consent; the only exceptions are brief quotations included in critical reviews and certain other noncommercial uses allowed by copyright law. This includes photocopying, recording, and other electronic or mechanical methods.

TABLE OF CONTENTS

INTRODUCTION

CHAPTER 1
Lip Balm 101: Everything You Need to Know.

LIP-SMACKING INGREDIENTS
TOOLS OF THE TRADE
MIXING AND MELTING TECHNIQUES
CUSTOMIZING YOUR CREATIONS

CHAPTER 2
Essential Supplies for Lip Balm Making

CHAPTER 3
Step-by-Step Guide to Creating Your Own Lip Balms.

HOW TO PREPARE LIP BALM AT HOME

CHAPTER 4
Advanced Lip Balm Recipes

MINT-CHOCOLATE LIP-BALM
STRAWBERRY LIP-BALM
ORANGE LIP-BALM
ROSE LIP-BALM
DIY VASELINE LIP-BALM
COCOA BUTTER LIP-BALM

CHAPTER 5
Where to Find the Best Resources and Supplies

CHAPTER 6
Personalizing Your Lip Balms: Scents, Flavors, and Colors.

CHAPTER 7
Troubleshooting Lip Balm Mishaps Like a Pro
HOW TO FIX A LIP BALM TUBE
REUSE YOUR LIP BALM: EASY SOLUTIONS & ADVICE.
HOW TO RESTORE MELTED LIP BALM
HOW TO MEND A BROKEN LIP BALM TUBE.
HOW TO REPAIR BROKEN LIP PRODUCTS.
TYPICAL LIP BALM ALLERGENS

CHAPTER 8
Packaging and Labeling Tips to Make Your Lip Balms Pop.

CHAPTER 9
Lip Balm Hacks and Expert Advice for Amazing Results

CHAPTER 10
Lip Balms for Every Season and Special Occasion

CONCLUSION

INTRODUCTION

WELCOME TO THE WORLD OF LIP BALMS

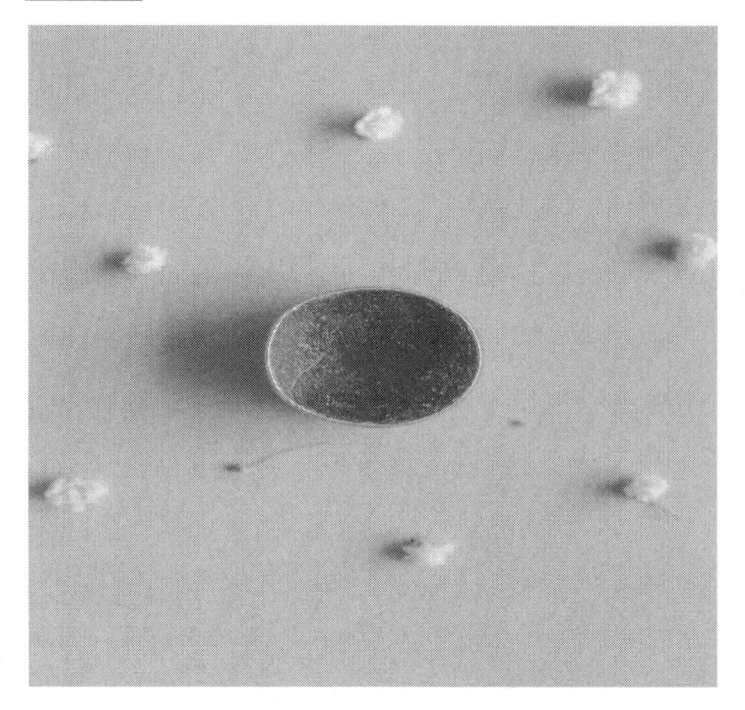

Have you ever pondered how to maintain kissable, silky, and soft lips? You don't need to go any further since this book is the best resource for learning how to make lip balms. Prepare yourself to explore a world of mouthwatering delights, regardless of your interests in DIY projects, beauty products, or becoming a successful business.

We'll get into the techniques for making your own lip balms in this book. We can help you with everything from knowing the components that give your lips a sumptuous sensation to learning sophisticated methods that will up the ante on lip balm. You will discover how to create customized lip balms that address various requirements, such adding a hint of color or SPF protection.

However, it doesn't end there. We'll also explore the fascinating worlds of lip balm marketing, packaging, and sales. Learn how to draw attention to your lip balms on the shelf and win over your consumers' hearts and lips. Also, to keep you ahead of the curve, we'll investigate the most recent developments and trends in the lip balm sector.

We'll solve any problems you run across along the way to make sure you master the art of creating lip balms. We'll also share success stories from other lip balm entrepreneurs who have successfully monetized their passions to motivate and encourage you.

So get your favorite lip balm, settle down, and join me as we set off on this thrilling journey. You'll have the know-how, abilities, and self-assurance to make lip balms that people will remember at the conclusion of this book. Let's nurture those lips so they're prepared for some major pouting!

Prepare to explore the world of lip balms, where indulgence meets inventiveness and endless amusement is in store. Now let's get going!

CHAPTER 1

Lip Balm 101: Everything You Need to Know.

In the opening chapter, we will build the basis for your study into the art of lip balm making. Get ready to learn about the basic materials, equipment, and methods that will enable you to become an expert in making beautiful lip balms.

LIP-SMACKING INGREDIENTS

We'll start by analyzing the fundamental elements that make lip balms oh-so-nourishing. From beeswax to shea butter, we'll find their distinct qualities and advantages. You'll learn how these components seal in moisture, protect your lips from harsh conditions, and leave you with a gorgeous pout.

BEESWAX: This organic wax, which comes from bees, is essential to lip balm magic. Your lips are protected from the elements by this barrier, which keeps moisture in and keeps out the elements like wind and cold. Additionally, beeswax contributes to the velvety, smooth feel that we all like in lip balms.

SHEA BUTTER: Rich and hydrating, shea butter is derived from the nuts of the shea tree and is a wonderful treatment for dry, chapped lips. Its abundant supply of vitamins and vital fatty acids helps moisturize and nourish your lips, leaving them feeling smooth and silky.

SWEET ALMOND OIL: This thin oil hydrates your lips deeply and keeps moisture from evaporating. It absorbs quickly. Additionally, it is high in vitamins and antioxidants, which will provide your lips an added layer of protection and nutrition.

COCONUT OIL: This all-natural moisturizer not only has a wonderful scent, but it also keeps your lips smooth and nourished. Rich in fatty acids, it supports good skin health and forms a barrier against dryness.

ESSENTIAL OILS: These fragrant oils give your lip balms a wonderful fragrance in addition to a host of other advantages. For instance, lavender oil may relax and soothe your lips, while peppermint oil might give you a cooling feeling. It is entirely up to you and your own tastes which essential oils you choose!

TOOLS OF THE TRADE

Let's explore the world of lip balm tools in this inquiry. From measuring spoons with accuracy to useful lip balm tubes, our all-inclusive coverage will provide you with the necessary tools to create your own custom lip balms. Learn about several molds, mixers, and packaging options that let you express your creativity and customize your lip balm recipes.

With the aid of these practical tools and materials, you can make lip balms that are not only amazing but also enjoyable to make.

MEASURING TOOLS: You'll need a digital scale or a pair of measuring spoons to guarantee accurate measures. These will assist you in measuring your components precisely so that your lip balms come out perfectly.

MIXING BOWLS: Gather a few mixing bowls that can withstand high temperatures. Glass or stainless steel bowls are quite useful. Having separate bowls makes it easier to combine batches or try out different tastes and hues.

DOUBLE BOILER OR MICROWAVE: There are two ways to melt materials evenly and softly. It works really well to use a double boiler configuration, which consists of placing a heatproof bowl over a pot of boiling water. An alternative is to cook your ingredients in a bowl that is safe to use in the microwave in brief bursts, stirring in between to prevent overheating.

STIRRING UTENSILS: A few spoons or spatulas that withstand heat will be your reliable allies when combining ingredients. They'll assist you in gently blending your components and making sure everything is mixed in.

LIP BALM TUBES OR CONTAINERS: You will obviously need a container to keep your lip balms! Due to its portability and ease of application, lip balm tubes are a popular option. If you would rather have a different style, you can also choose tiny jars or tins. Remember to keep enough on hand to store all of your creations of lip balm!

FUNNEL: You can pour your lip balm mixture into tubes or containers with ease if you have a tiny funnel. It guarantees a clean and orderly filling procedure and lessens spills.

LABELS AND PACKAGING SUPPLIES: To give your work an additional professional and customized touch, pick up some labels and packaging supplies. Either create your own label design or purchase pre-made labels online. To really personalize your lip balms, think about attaching adorable stickers, ribbons, or even handwritten notes.

These are just the fundamentals; as your skill at creating lip balms increases, you can always get inventive and experiment with other supplies. Finding the right tool for you requires some experimentation and fun, so make sure to do both.

MIXING AND MELTING TECHNIQUES

You'll get professional advice on how to melt and blend the ingredients for your lip balm. Learn the best methods for producing a smooth, creamy texture that ensures your lip balms apply flawlessly. You will receive invaluable expert advice on how to avoid common pitfalls and create lip balms that have an alluringly dreamy appearance.

we'll go into the fascinating realm of blending and melting methods for creating your own lip balms. Prepare to go on the delightful journey of crafting your own lip balm recipes!

There are a few methods you may use to combine the components for homemade lip balm. The twin boiler approach is one that is often used. This is placing your components in a heat-safe dish or container on top of a saucepan of boiling water.

Your components will melt gently and evenly under the steam's mild heat, resulting in a smooth and well-blended lip balm formulation.

Don't worry if you don't have a double boiler! A temporary one may be made by putting a glass bowl or container that is safe for high heat over a saucepan of boiling water. Just watch out that your ingredients don't become overheated by touching the water with the bottom of the dish.

You may also try using a microwave as a method. Put all of the components for your lip balm in a microwave-safe container and heat them briefly, stirring in between, until everything is melted and well mixed. Avoid overheating the mixture as this may lead to the oils separating or become too hot to handle.

It's time to transfer your components into your lip balm containers when they have melted and blended. To guarantee a precise and mess-free transfer, use a dropper or a tiny funnel. Allowing a little margin for the lip balm to firm and settle, fill each container nearly to the brim.

As the lip balm mixture cools, it may begin to thicken, so proceed with caution and speed while mixing and pouring. If you discover that your mixture is hardening too rapidly, you may use the previously described techniques to slowly reheat it.

FLAVOR AND FRAGRANCE FUN

Who said lip balm had to be boring? We'll delve into the realm of tastes and smells in this part. You'll discover how to add mouthwatering flavors and smells to your lip balms that will make your lips appealing, ranging from traditional favorites like vanilla and mint to more daring choices like tropical fruits or even chocolate chip cookie dough.

By adding delicious flavors and smells to your lip balm creations, this area will elevate them to a whole new level and make your lips pucker with enjoyment. Prepare to have your senses teased!

TASTING TASTES: The possibilities are endless when it comes to tastes! Choose from traditional favorites like vanilla, strawberry, or mint, or try something different with tastes like cotton candy, bubblegum, or watermelon. Imagine turning your favorite sweets into lip balms by thinking about them. You have many options, including the ability to combine different tastes to make your own distinctive concoction.

FRAGRANCE FANTASIES: Alright, let's discuss scents now. Similar to tastes, you can customize your lip balms with a variety of aromas to give them an additional luxurious feel. Picture the zest of crisp citrus, the tropical flavor of coconut, or the soothing smell of lavender. Even try experimenting with flowery tones, such as jasmine or rose. The secret is to choose scents that elevate your spirits and make you feel amazing.

BALANCING ACT: It's crucial to find a balance when choosing scents and tastes. Your lip balms should taste and smell fantastic without being too so. To get the required strength, start with a little quantity of flavor or fragrance oil and progressively increase it. Keep in mind that a little goes a long way, so begin lightly and make adjustments as necessary.

QUALITY IS IMPORTANT: When it comes to fragrance and flavor oils, quality is crucial. Because they are safe to use on your sensitive lips, look for oils that are particularly made for preparing lip balms. These oils often have a strong, enduring flavor or aroma because of their high concentration. To make sure you're obtaining the highest quality oils for your lip balms, be sure to check reviews and choose reliable sources.

MIXING MAGIC: Timing is everything when it comes to adding taste and scent to your lip balm concoction. The time to add them is after your basic components, like oils and beeswax, have melted together, during the melting and mixing phase. This guarantees a uniform distribution of tastes and scents throughout your lip balms by allowing them to mix in perfectly with the mixture.

CUSTOMIZING YOUR CREATIONS

I'll inspire you to release your inner artist and design your lip balms. We'll offer ideas for adding color, sparkle, or even SPF protection to your works. Get ready to build lip balms that represent your own personality and flair.

As your guide, I'll walk you through the process of adding your own touch to make your lip balms really unique. Prepare to let your creativity run wild and create lip balms that perfectly capture your own aesthetic!

VIBRANT CREATIONS: Adding a pop of color is one of the simplest ways to personalize your lip balms. A wide range of lip-safe colorants are available, including liquid colors, mica powders, and even natural components like cocoa or beetroot powder. Try experimenting with various hues to make lip balms that go with your attire or your mood. Just keep in mind that you should add more slowly at first until you reach the appropriate level of color intensity.

SHINE AND SPARKLE: Who doesn't like a little shine? Use glitter or shimmer to give your lip balms a glamorous touch. It is okay to apply mica powders or glitters of cosmetic quality on your lips. Your lip balms may reach new heights of fabulousness with a dash of glitter, whether you choose for a subtle sheen or a spectacular dazzle.

INGENIOUS CONTAINERS: Packaging is important to remember! Your choice of lip balm container might be just as crucial as the balm itself. Look at several possibilities such as adorable tins, elegant tubes, or even tiny jars. Examine the container's dimensions, design, and capacity. You want something that is useful for daily usage in addition to having a gorgeous appearance. To locate distinctive containers that best represent your own style, use your imagination and creativity.

LABEL LOVE: Adding labels to your lip balms lets you further customize them while also giving them a more polished appearance. Use graphic design tools to create your own labels, or get inventive and handwrite some labels. Add the ingredients list, the name of your lip balm, and any other details you would want to contribute. Even better, you may personalize it with a humorous phrase or adorable picture. Adding labels to your lip balms may help them seem presentable and ready to be given as gifts or shared.

SMELL-SATIONAL COMBINATIONS: Flavors and scents have previously been discussed, so why not go one step further and develop original smell combinations? Create your own distinctive smells by combining various essential oils or fragrance oils. For instance, you may mix coconut and vanilla for better smell.

CHAPTER 2

Essential Supplies for Lip Balm Making

With the correct tools, making your own lip balm is a gratifying and enjoyable project that can be completed relatively easily. The following are the necessities for you to have:

BASIC SUBSTANCES

Your lip balm's primary structural ingredient, beeswax, gives it a thick viscosity and shields your lips. Beeswax is available in bricks, pellets, or grated form for convenient measurement. Pellets of beeswax.

CARRIER OILS: Your lips will get hydration and nourishment from these oils. Olive oil, jojoba oil, almond oil, and coconut oil are common options. When selecting an oil for your lip balm, make sure it is food-grade and absorbs easily. coconut oil.

BUTTERS: Butters give your lip balm even more richness and hydrating power. Although shea and cocoa butter are well-liked choices, you may also try mango or avocado butter. Shea butter.

ADD-ON INGREDIENTS

ESSENTIAL OILS: These oils provide your lip balm taste and aroma. Lavender is recognized for its relaxing qualities, while peppermint is a popular option for its cooling impact. Tea tree oil, lemon, grapefruit, and vanilla oils are further choices. Just remember that essential oils may be powerful, so use them wisely. essential oil of peppermint.

COLORANTS: Natural colorants like mica powder or cocoa powder may be used to add a hint of color to your lip balm. Start with a tiny bit and add more until you have the desired hue since a little goes a long way. powdered mica.

SWEETENERS: You may use a little amount of agave nectar, stevia, or honey to give your lip balm a somewhat sweet flavor.

INSTRUMENTS AND APPARATUS

HEAT-SAFE BOWL OR DOUBLE BOILER:

This is what you'll need to slowly melt your components.

Measure measuring cups and spoons to ensure precise measures.

Use a whisk or spatula to mix your items.

TINY GLASS OR METAL BOWLS: To contain your melted components and to combine with extra colorants or flavorings.

LIP BALM CONTAINERS: A range of sizes are available in tubes, tins, or pots. Verify if they are airtight and impermeable. tubes of lip balm.

LABELS (OPTIONAL): You may personalize your lip balm with labels if you're selling it or giving it as a gift.

EXTRA ADVICE: Use low heat to melt your components; avoid letting the mixture boil.
Allow the lip balm to cool fully before including any colorants or essential oils.
Keep your lip balm somewhere cold and dark.
Play around with tastes and ingredients to see what works best!

These basic ingredients combined with a little imagination will allow you to create healthful and tasty lip balms that you can give as presents to loved ones or enjoy yourself.

CHAPTER 3

Step-by-Step Guide to Creating Your Own Lip Balms.

Natural lip balm is simple to make and enjoyable to make. It provides you complete control over what gets on your kisser and just needs a few components! For a special occasion, homemade lip balm is a wonderful and practical handmade present to give to friends, coworkers, or loved ones.

Use much the same formula as for the organic lip balms, follow along to find out precisely how to produce moisturizing homemade lip balm.

HOW TO PREPARE LIP BALM AT HOME

SUPPLIES REQUIRED

Two Boilers. Alternatively, nestle a smaller pot, heat-safe glass bowl, or stainless steel bowl within a bigger pot to form animprovised double boiler.

Tiny receptacles to preserve your last batch of handmade lip balm.

Think about choices such as these Tins weighing 1/2 ounce, 1 ounce, and much smaller.Tiny glass jars, cardboard chapstick tubes, or 15-ounce plastic tubes might work well.

A glass measuring cup or other comparable smaller bowl/pitcher with a pour spout is optional.

COMPONENTS

One part bee wax. Since beeswax pastilles are the simplest to work with, I suggest using them. Refer to the following remarks about beeswax replacement.

One part cocoa butter. Wafers made of cocoa butter are a well-liked option that are also simple to use.

Mango or shea butter might also work well. We really like the aromas of rich chocolate that cocoa butter brings to our all-natural lip balms!

Two parts premium edible oil. You are welcome to blend a few different oils together. If pressed for time, my first pick would be organic sweet almond oil. It has a very subtle taste and aroma, is nutrient-rich, and very hydrating.

ESSENTIAL OILS (OPTIONAL).

The ingredient are listed in "parts" (by volume) so you could easily adjust the recipe for natural lip balm to your preferred strength. For example, to make around 12 ounces of lip balm, combine 1/2 cup beeswax, ½ cup cocoa butter, and 1 cup oil. Alternatively, for a much smaller amount, mix 2 teaspoons of oil with 1 tablespoon each of cocoa butter and beeswax.

TIP: Use one part beeswax, one part cocoa butter, and four parts oil (e.g., 60 grams beeswax, 60 grams cocoa butter, and 240 grams oil) to measure by weight rather than volume.

A dappled brown and black wooden board displays the components for making homemade lip balm, along with a white bowl of oil, a white ramekin filled with pastilles made of beeswax, and a white ramekin filled with wafers made of cocoa butter. Beside the components comes a little vial of organic sweet orange essential oil.

One part beeswax, one part cocoa butter, and two parts oil by volume (or 1:1:4 by weight) are the essential components of handmade lip balm.

You may add essential oils to your DIY lip balm recipe, but be sure you use only premium "edible" oils. The preferable option is organic.

Popular essential oils used to flavor natural lip balms include:

- Jasmine
- Chamomile
- Sweet orange
- Pink grapefruit
- Spearmint
- Wintergreen
- Peppermint.

Please be aware that certain citrus essential oils, including bergamot, lemon, and lime, are deemed "phototoxic," which means they raise the possibility of being sunburned when exposed to direct sunlight. This is usually a problem, however, when skin is directly exposed to extremely high or undiluted amounts of citrus oil. Sweet oranges don't cause phytotoxicity.

Use up to 96 drops (1 light tsp) of essential oils for every cup of oil used, at most, to create a lip balm with a pretty strong aroma. Resized, it equates to 12 drops of essential oils for every 2 tablespoons of base oil. Use roughly half the quantity to produce lip balm with a softer smell.

Plan Therapy Essential Oils are shown in four bottles: one each of Organic Sweet Orange, Organic Peppermint, Organic Lavender, and a smaller container of Organic Pink Grapefruit.

KIND OF OIL THAT WORKS BEST FOR MAKING HOMEMADE LIP BALM

Any high-quality edible oil, such as hemp seed oil, sweet almond oil, olive oil, fractionated (liquid) coconut oil, sunflower oil, avocado oil, or anything similar, may be used to produce lip balm. Since the texture of solidified coconut oil changes greatly with temperature, it might be more difficult to correct. Be aware that strong or distinct-flavored oils (such coconut or olive) will affect the overall taste and scent of your homemade lip balm.

Even though lip balm is a "cosmetic," I personally steer clear of utilizing oils that are labeled as "cosmetic use only" (such as rosehip seed oil or argan oil) since the finished product will be quite close to your mouth. Still, they are excellent options for recipes with calendula, cannabis, or lavender body salve!

A double boiler is placed on top of a gas stove. The components for making homemade lip balm are situated on a butcher block countertop to the right. There is also a glass measuring cup of oil, twelve one-ounce metal tins, a white ramekin filled with beeswax pastilles, and sweet orange essential oil.

HOW TO PREPARE LIP BALM AT HOME

Before you begin, make sure all of your materials and components are prepared.

Add the oil, wax, and cocoa or shea butter to the upper part of a double boiler after weighing or measuring them. Make sure there is enough water in the lower half of the double boiler so that the top pan is submerged in water. Although a little difficult, measuring cocoa wafers in cups is nevertheless effective! For instance, we discovered that the weight of half a cup of cocoa butter wafers and half a cup of beeswax is around 60 grams each.

The ingredients should be heated to a thorough melting and combining point over medium-high heat. Stir from time to time. When heating, do not cover the pot since this can allow condensation to form, which might damage your lip balm.

Before adding the essential oils, turn off the heat and take the saucepan out of the oven. Due to their inherent volatility, essential oils will evaporate rapidly when heated to a high temperature.

Gently transfer the liquid into your preferred lip balm containers while it's still hot. If you have a glass measuring cup on hand, it's best to pour the melted substance from the double-boiler into tiny lip balm containers after transferring it there, in batches if necessary. To stop the mixture from cooling too rapidly or from sticking when it comes into touch with the cold glass, microwave the glass measuring cup for 30 seconds beforehand. Just put it back on the stove to remelt if the mixture begins to solidify before you're done pouring.

Add labels and lids when the lip balm has fully cooled and solidified.

Savor your lips with hydration and suppleness, and spread the word to your friends.

CLEANING ADVICE: Wipe the pan out right away with a paper towel for the simplest cleanup. Should the lip balm residue begin to solidify inside the pan, gently reheat it to facilitate further melting.

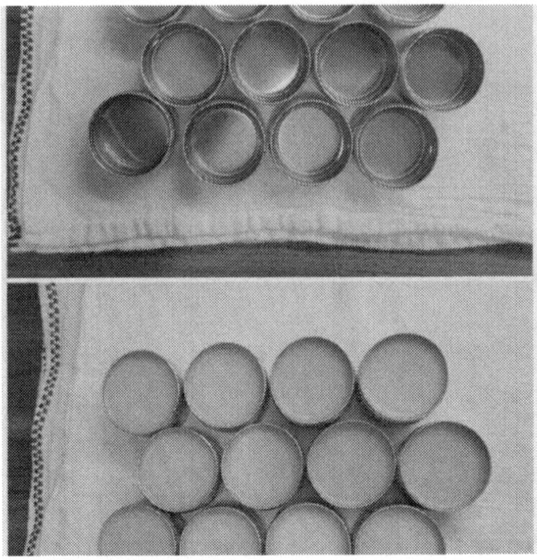

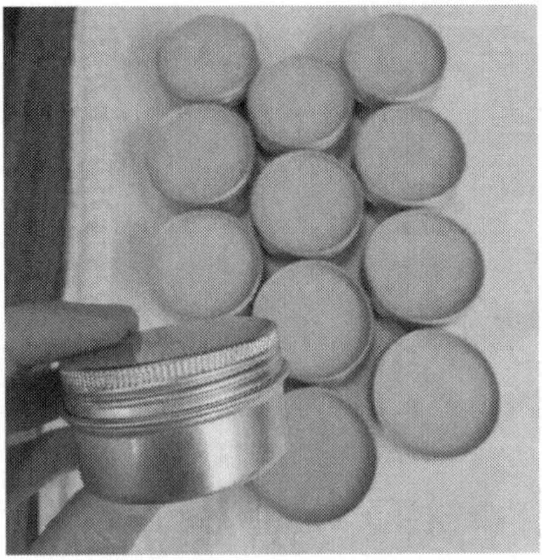

CHAPTER 4

Advanced Lip Balm Recipes

Take a look at how to make your own luxurious lip balm at home. We think creating skincare products in your home is superior than purchasing them from stores as you may be in complete control of the components.

This procedure gives you the ability to customize the final result to fit your tastes while also giving you more control. It's time to say goodbye to traditional lip stains and welcome lip balms as the new main attraction.

Discover the craft of creating a custom lip balm, and get tips on how to become an expert at it here.

MINT-CHOCOLATE LIP-BALM

You need four ingredients to prepare this lip-balm:

- ☐ 1 teaspoon of cocoa powder

- ☐ 2 tablespoons of coconut oil

- ☐ 2 teaspoons of white beeswax pellets

- ☐ 4-5 drops of peppermint oil

HERE'S HOW TO PREPARE IT

Beeswax pellets should be melted in a stovetop boiler.

After it has melted, thoroughly whisk in some cocoa powder.

Stir well after adding a few drops of almond and peppermint oils to the mixture.

Before putting the mixture in a jar, turn off the heat and allow it to cool.

Place it in the refrigerator to solidify when it has cooled.

STRAWBERRY LIP-BALM

You need four ingredients to prepare this lip-balm:

☐ 1 tablespoon of shea butter

☐ 2 tablespoons of coconut oil

☐ 2-3 drops of orange essential oil

☐ 1 tablespoon of beeswax

HERE'S HOW TO PREPARE IT

Pour a tiny amount of water into a pan and set it over low to medium heat in a double boiler.

Put some beeswax and shea butter in the cup and let it to melt.

Mix in a little amount of coconut oil and whisk well.

When everything has melted, remove the liquid from the heat and stir in the orange essential oil.

After giving everything a good stir, pour the mixture into a jar or other container.

After letting it cool for 30 minutes, you're done.

ORANGE LIP-BALM

You need four ingredients to prepare this lip-balm:

☐ 1 tablespoon of shea butter

☐ 2 tablespoons of coconut oil

☐ 2-3 drops of orange essential oil

☐ 1 tablespoon of beeswax

HERE'S HOW TO PREPARE IT

Pour a tiny amount of water into a pan and set it over low to medium heat in a double boiler.

Put some beeswax and shea butter in the cup and let it melt.

Mix in a little amount of coconut oil and whisk well.

When everything has melted, remove the liquid from the heat and stir in the orange essential oil.

After giving everything a good stir, pour the mixture into a jar or other container.

After letting it cool for 30 minutes, you're done.

ROSE LIP-BALM

You need four ingredients to prepare this lip-balm:

- ☐ 1 tablespoon of shea butter

- ☐ 1 tablespoon of beeswax

- ☐ 2 tablespoons of coconut oil

- ☐ 2-3 drops of rose essential oil

HERE'S HOW TO PREPARE IT

Shea butter, beeswax, and coconut oil should all be combined in a skillet and heated to a double boil.

After stirring and allowing the ingredients to melt, transfer the mixture into a jar or other container.

After adding a few drops of rose essential oil, let the mixture cool for thirty minutes.

DIY VASELINE LIP-BALM

You need three ingredients to prepare this lip-balm:

- ☐ 1 ½ tablespoon of Vaseline (or any petroleum jelly)
- ☐ ½ tablespoon of beetroot juice
- ☐ ½ tablespoon of honey

HERE'S HOW TO PREPARE IT

In a jar, combine a little amount of honey and Vaseline.

Pour in the beetroot juice. The components shouldn't be mixed together.

Microwave the container for about 30 seconds.

Take it out of the microwave, mix everything together, put it in a pan, and let it sit for half an hour.

COCOA BUTTER LIP-BALM

You need four ingredients to prepare this lip-balm:

- ☐ 10 grams of beeswax

- ☐ 20 grams of cocoa butter

- ☐ 20 grams of coconut oil

- ☐ 5 drops of an essential oil of your choice

HERE'S HOW TO PREPARE IT

In a double boiler, melt a little amount of beeswax.

Add a little amount of cocoa butter to the pan after the majority of it has melted, and mix the two together.

Make sure there are no lumps when you add a few drops of coconut oil to the pan after the two have melted.

Remove the liquid from the heat and stir in a few drops of essential oil (It may be lavender or another kind).

Pour everything into a jar and let it cool for around thirty minutes.

CHAPTER 5

Where to Find the Best Resources and Supplies

To make your own lip balm, it's important to have the proper tools and equipment. Fortunately, you can get everything you need to make your own amazing lip balms in a lot of locations!

Your neighborhood craft shop is a fantastic alternative. These shops often have an area just for do-it-yourself cosmetics, such as ingredients for making lip balm. Many necessary components, such as shea butter, beeswax, and other oils, may be found to give your lip balm its ideal texture and nourishing qualities. Also, they often offer a variety of adorable labels and packaging to give your lip balms a more fashionable appearance!

If you're more of an internet shopper, there are many websites that offer materials and ingredients for lip balms. These internet retailers provide a large assortment of premium ingredients that are imported from across the globe. You may experiment with various tastes, hues, and even unique components like vitamin additions or natural extracts. You may get anything you need delivered straight to your house with only a few clicks.

Here are some websites that specialize in selling lip balm ingredients and supplies:

1. *BRAMBLEBERRY*: www.brambleberry.com

2. *BULKAPOTHECARY*: www.bulkapothecary.com

3. ***WHOLESALESUPPLIESPLUS***:www.wholesalesuppliesplus.com

4. ***ESSENTIALWHOLESALE&LABS***:www.essentialwholesale.com

5. ***NEWDIRECTIONSAROMATICS***:www.newdirectionsaromatics.com

NOTE: Always ensure to check the reliability and reviews of the suppliers before making any purchases.

Joining forums or groups for do-it-yourself beauty is another option to think about. Enthusiastic lip balm fans populate these groups, and they are always delighted to recommend their preferred vendors and resources. Not only can you uncover new ingredients and learn from their experiences, but you may also get ideas for creative packaging. It's a fantastic opportunity to learn from and network with other lip balm manufacturers.

Here are some DIY beauty communities and forums where passionate lip balm enthusiasts often share their experiences and tips:

1. ***THE DISH FORUM BY SWIFT CRAFTY MONKEY:*** [www.swiftcraftymonkey.blog](https://swiftcraftymonkey.blog/the-dish/)

2. ***SOAP MAKING FORUM:*** www.soapmakingforum.com

3. *MAKING SKINCARE COMMUNITY*: [www.makingskincare.com](https://www.makingskincare.com/community/)

4. *LOTIONCRAFTER FORUM:* [www.lotioncrafter.com](https://www.lotioncrafter.com/forum/)

5. *CURLYNIKKI FORUMS (DIY SECTION):* www.curlynikkiforums.com

These communities are great places to connect with fellow DIY beauty enthusiasts, share ideas, and gather insights for creating your own lip balm formulations.

Don't overlook your neighborhood's specialized stores or farmers' markets. Handmade skincare sellers, such as those selling lip balms, are often found in these locales. You can boost the local economy in your town and have access to premium ingredients by patronizing local companies.

It's an interesting quest to discover the finest ingredients and resources for lip balm creation. A plethora of opportunities await you to manufacture the most incredible lip balms ever—whether you peruse the aisles of a craft store, peruse internet stores, connect with communities, or patronize nearby companies!

CHAPTER 6

Personalizing Your Lip Balms: Scents, Flavors, and Colors

Customizing your lip balms with distinctive tastes, fragrances, and colors is one of the most imaginative and enjoyable parts of making your own. This chapter will walk you through the process of giving your handmade lip balms a little additional flair!

SMELLS: A lip balm's aroma may take you to a delightfully sensual realm. There are many different scent alternatives available, including zesty citrus, relaxing lavender, exotic coconut, and refreshing peppermint. Try out several essential oils or fragrance oils to discover the ideal aroma that complements your preferences and attitude.

Applying lip balm may be made really enjoyable by even a little trace of these lovely scents.

TASTE: Who said lip balm had to be uninteresting? Adding delectable scents to your lip balms might enhance their use. Imagine how satisfying it would be to apply lip balm that tastes like rich vanilla, juicy watermelon, or sweet strawberry. You may experiment with different food-grade flavorings or natural ingredients to develop lip balms that will satisfy your palate and make your lips feel pampered.

COLORS: You may enhance the visual appeal and allure of your lip balms by adding a hint of color to them. Try experimenting with other natural colorants, such as cocoa powder for a warm brown tint, spirulina powder for a cool green tone, or powdered beetroot for a soft pink tint. Your lip balms may still be healthy while adding a beautiful shade with just a little bit of these natural colorants.

Keep in mind that the key to customizing your lip balms is to use your imagination and give them a distinctive personality. It's okay to combine different tastes, smells, and colors to create your own unique line of lip balms. Even your favorite foods, sweets, or locations might serve as inspiration. There are many options!

Remember that it's crucial to utilize substances that are safe for your skin and lips as you set off on your voyage of customisation. Make sure the tastes, fragrances, and colorants you choose are appropriate for use in lip cosmetics at all times.

So feel free to let your creativity go wild! Make lip balms that will make you grin every time you use them, in addition to keeping your lips hydrated.

CHAPTER 7

Troubleshooting Lip Balm Mishaps Like a Pro

You're not alone if you've ever tried applying lip balm and found that it won't slide down, leaving you frustrated. This is a typical issue that many have had, and it can be quite annoying while attempting to maintain the moisture level of your lips. Thankfully, you can get your lip balm sliding down again with a few easy steps.

You may restore your lip balm to its previous functioning condition by warming it up, wiping it off, or even shaking it around. You can quickly get your lip balm sliding down again with a little bit of work.

According to Zeichner, if these formulations are used too often, they create an artificial barrier to lock in moisture, which makes lips sluggish since the skin can't keep itself hydrated. Instead, she suggests that you progressively decrease the amount of lip balm you use and that you accept some

HOW TO FIX A LIP BALM TUBE

To make sure the grip is properly tightened, it might be required to twist the tube up or down. Make a twisted form out of the lip balm if you have a lot of it. To make it harder to twist if you don't have much, twist it a little higher. Covering the little stick within the tube is the primary way to keep it in place.

REUSE YOUR LIP BALM: EASY SOLUTIONS & ADVICE.

Lip balm is a crucial component of lip protection, but when it runs out or melts, leaving you with a tube of bare lips, it may be hard to find. You can immediately fix and repurpose your lip balm by using a few easy tips. If a lip balm tube breaks, let it air dry for a full thirty seconds before putting it back on its feet.

As a consequence of the melt, the chapstick will melt and be able to return to the chamber. It will be as good as new after it has hardened. To remelt the wax into the tube, just microwave the chapstick for a little while once it has melted.

It will harden again into its natural condition as it cools. Your lip balm tube should last anywhere from six to twelve months, depending on the contents and packaging. It is feasible to recycle the used lip balm tube if one has to be replaced. After boiling the tubes, use a cotton bud to remove any remaining waxy residue. If you take the time to take care of your lip balm tubes, you may extend their lifespan.

HOW TO RESTORE MELTED LIP BALM

It's simple to repair melted lip balm! To solidify the balm, first put it in the freezer for a few hours. After it has solidified, you may remove the top layer of melted wax with a knife and dispose of it.

The balm may then be placed in a container that will prevent it from melting again. You may cover it with foil or plastic wrap if you don't have a container that can keep it chilly. You're done when you put the lip balm in a cold, dry location!

HOW TO MEND A BROKEN LIP BALM TUBE.

You'll need some wax paper, scissors, and a lighter to mend a cracked lip balm tube. First, trim the tube's top just below the fractured area. After that, use the lighter and gently heat the tube's cut edge. Press down hard after placing the wax paper exactly over the hot edge.

By sealing the tube, this should restore its use. Now you may enjoy it once again by filling the tube with your preferred lip balm.

HOW TO REPAIR BROKEN LIP PRODUCTS.

Because lip cosmetics might melt or crack, handling them is quite challenging. There are a few easy fixes you may try if your lip liner breaks or melts. You need to warm up a metal spoon in hot water before you start. After the spoon reaches the boiling point, carefully push the fragmented liner pieces back together until a single, solid piece forms. Vaseline or lip balm applied in a tiny quantity will hold the components together.

Chapsticks that have melted in your pocket may be put back where they belong by giving them a little microwave cooking. Subsequently, the wax will solidify and melt back into the tube.

It is advised to keep ChapStick® products between 20–25 C (68–77 F) after opening and using them for a year, even though they do not expire. To repurpose used lip balm tubes, start by using a cotton bud to extract as much of the remaining wax as you can. Boil the tube and remove any leftovers before using it again.

TYPICAL LIP BALM ALLERGENS

Lip balm base chemicals, scents, and additions are examples of common lip balm irritants. The most often occurring substances that might irritate skin are

- Phenol
- Lanolin
- Parabens
- Camphor
- Menthol

These components may result in burning, irritation, swelling, and dryness. In addition, artificial colorings used to lip balms to enhance their appearance and various scents added to give them a scent might irritate skin.

It's critical to review the lip balm's ingredients list and stay away from any known irritants. It's advisable to stop using lip balm and see a doctor if you encounter any negative side effects.

For a mild, hydrating remedy for dry, chapped lips, apply lip balms and other lip cosmetics. You should be warned, however, that some items' components might be harmful to your health.

It is not advisable to use lip balms that include menthol, camphor, phenol, or any other alcohol-containing material. While these substances may provide a cooling effect right away, they may also cause skin irritation and even peel off the skin's surface layers, leaving lips vulnerable to environmental harm.

Similar to this, parents need to be aware of the hazards if their kid ingests lip cosmetics, even if the majority of them are safe. The number to call IPC is 1-800-222-1222. You should take your kid to the doctor if they start throwing up.

Therefore, it is important to properly label and supervise all lip cosmetics with consideration for the safety of children.

CHAPTER 8

Packaging and Labeling Tips to Make Your Lip Balms Pop.

We'll go into the fascinating realm of packaging and labeling in this chapter, where you may draw attention to your lip balms and make them stand out from the crowd.

PACKAGING: Choosing the appropriate packaging may have a significant impact on how people see your lip balms. Think of using adorable and striking packaging that matches the topic of your lip balm collection or your own particular taste.

For a touch of elegance, you may use vintage lip balm tubes, beautiful tin containers, or even little glass jars. Remember to make sure the packaging is strong and secure to keep your lip balms safe.

LABELING: Your lip balms may seem polished and enticing with a well-designed label. Start by coming up with a distinctive design or logo that embodies your company or sense of style. For an added personal touch, you may hand-draw your labels or utilize graphic design tools.

Don't forget to include crucial facts like the brand name of your lip balm, the components that went into it, and any other specifics like the taste or aroma. Think about using eye-catching typefaces and colors that complement the overall design of your lip balms.

When applying the labels, ensure sure the package is properly aligned and the labels are centered. If the packaging permits, you may even print directly onto it or utilize sticky labels. Your lip balms will look professional and stay fresh and tamper-proof if you add a transparent protective seal or shrink wrap.

Think about using a few additional details to elevate your packaging and labeling. If you want to give your lip balms as gifts, you may make unique gift tags, fasten a little charm or sticker to the container, or wrap the lip balm tubes in vibrant ribbon. Your lip balms may feel like a special treat with these little touches.

Labeling and packaging have functional uses in addition to being aesthetically pleasing. Secure packaging keeps your lip balms safe and clean while clear and informative labeling lets clients know what they're purchasing.

CHAPTER 9

Lip Balm Hacks and Expert Advice for Amazing Results

1. PREPARE YOUR LIPS: Make sure your lips are ready and prepared before using lip balm. Use a gentle toothbrush or a homemade sugar and honey scrub to gently exfoliate them. This will eliminate any flaky areas on your lips, leaving them smooth and primed for lip balm application.

2. DRINK WATER FROM THE INSIDE OUT: Happy lips are hydrated lips! In order to keep your lips hydrated from the inside out, make sure you drink plenty of water throughout the day. This will enhance the benefits of your lip balm and leave your lips looking lush and full.

3. NOURISHMENT AT NIGHT: Right before bed is one of the ideal times to offer your lips a little more love and care. Before you turn in for the night, apply a thick layer of lip balm and let it to do its job. Your lips will be moisturized and silky when you wake up.

4. SUN PROTECTION: Your lips need protection from the sun's damaging rays, just like your skin. Seek for a lip balm with a minimum SPF of 15 or above. This will protect your lips from UV rays and maintain their youthful appearance.

5. ALL-AROUND SUPERHERO: Lip balm isn't limited to your lips! It may also be used for other purposes. Use it to tame those annoying flyaway hairs, treat minor burns or bug bites, and nourish dry cuticles. Similar like having a little superhero in your pocket!

6. LAYER UP: Applying many layers of lip balm will really hydrate your lips if they're feeling particularly parched or dry. After allowing the first thin coating to absorb, add a second layer. By doing this, you'll build a barrier of defense and retain the moisture for sustained hydration.

7. LESS IS MORE: Although it may be tempting to reapply lip balm many times throughout the day, keep in mind that a little amount goes a long way. Applying too much balm might actually cause your lips to become dependent on it and stop them from retaining moisture naturally. Don't overdo it; only use it when necessary.

8. REMAIN CONSISTENT: When it comes to lip balm, consistency is essential. To keep your lips feeling supple and moisturized, include it into your daily routine and use it often.

CHAPTER 10

Lip Balms for Every Season and Special Occasion

1. WINTER WONDERLAND: Use a lip balm that offers great hydration and wind protection when the weather becomes cold. For hydrated lips that resist drying out and chapping, look for ingredients like shea butter, beeswax, or coconut oil.

2. SPRING FLING: Use a lighter lip balm with a dash of color when the weather warms and the flowers blossom. With the added moisture of tinted lip balms, your lips will seem more youthful and natural. Select hues that go well with your skin tone and appreciate spring's beauty.

3. SUMMER VIBES: It's important to shield your lips from damaging UV rays when the sun is blazing and you're spending more time outside. Choose a lip balm with an SPF of at least 30, if possible. Seek for lip balms with light compositions so you can fully enjoy those bright days without feeling heavy on your lips.

4. AUTUMN DELIGHT: Look for lip balms with nourishing ingredients like vitamin E or jojoba oil when the leaves begin to turn color and the air becomes brisk. These will alleviate any dryness brought on by the shifting climate. Use lip balms with earthy, warm tones to embrace the homey atmosphere of fall.

5. SPECIAL OCCASIONS: Use a lip balm with a hint of glitz for those special occasions or evenings out. To accentuate your inherent beauty, look for lip balms with a glossy finish or a hint of glitter. For every event, you'll feel confident and ready to dazzle.

CONCLUSION

This marks the conclusion of our lip balm journey! We've looked at lip care, covering everything from the fundamentals of lip balm to its incredible advantages and different tricks.

We now know how to choose the ideal lip balm for various times of the year and special events. I really hope that this book has been beneficial to you and has motivated you to take better care of your lips.

Recall that lip balm is an essential for maintaining healthy, hydrated, and smackable lips—it's not simply a cosmetic! Therefore, regardless of the time of year or event, remember to include lip balm in your daily regimen. Your lips will appreciate the gesture!

Please feel free to ask any further lip balm-related questions or for a reminder at the review, and I'll do my best to address them in my next book.

Made in the USA
Columbia, SC
12 February 2025